12 Questions

Life Experiments to Expand Your Heart & Mind

Dr. Bernard Bull

Birdhouse Learning Labs, LLC
11561 North Buntrock Avenue
Mequon, WI 53092
www.birdhouselearninglabs.com

Printed in the United States of America

Cover by Riki Unrau.

ISBN 978-1-7333201-1-5

Library of Congress Control Number: 2019948648

First Edition

DISCLAIMER

This book is not intended as a substitute for the advice from a mental health or other healthcare professional. The reader should consult an appropriate professional in matters relating to mental and physical health. The publisher and author do not make any warranties about the completeness, reliability, and accuracy of this information. Any action you take based upon the contents of this book is strictly at your own risk. Neither the author nor the publisher claims responsibility for adverse effects resulting from the life experiments or information found within this book.

CONTENTS

INTRODUCTION

At 36-years old, I received one of the most precious gifts of my life. Looking into my newborn son's eyes, I felt immense joy. But when I saw a reflection of myself holding my new son, something else was triggered. In that reflection I saw another person. I saw my father.

When I was born, my father was a 37-year-old man, a small business owner, a husband, and a new father. But he didn't look like a 37-year-old man. He was already showing signs of serious heart problems, intensified by harmful lifestyle choices. Twelve years after my birth, after he made it through multiple heart attacks and a stroke, I found myself in the back seat of the van as my mother raced my dad to the hospital in the middle of the night. Everything that followed lasted only an hour, but it felt like that hour stretched on for several days. We arrived at the hospital; we were in his room; the doctors and staff rushed in and out. I watched as my father died of a massive heart attack.

I looked away from that mirror, away from that memory, and looked at this beautiful new child in my arms. I cried. They were tears of joy and fear. A heavy weight settled onto my chest and sunk down into my stomach. A disorienting fog crept into my mind.

I did not want to follow my father's path.

I wanted my son to grow up with a dad who was there for him during his splendid but tumultuous teen years as he explored the possibilities for his own life. I wanted him to experience life with a father who was present, who loved him, and who experienced his joys and challenges by his side. Most of all, I didn't want him to grow up haunted by vivid and unrelenting memories of a dead dad, memories like mine – a young man in a hospital waiting room, stunned, shivering, tearless, empty, and beyond emotion.

Little did I know, like the Greek myths of old, I cursed myself to start down the road that lead to my father's untimely death. It was a path that took control of my life and nearly destroyed me.

Over the years that followed, that fear grew. I experienced migraines off and on for a long time, but they suddenly started coming several times a week, leaving me exhausted and depressed, struggling to be emotionally present for those around me. My productivity at work declined. I binged on fitness and random diets, seeking ways to add a few more years to my life, while almost always giving up and falling into unhealthy habits. I developed seemingly random fears and anxieties, like convincing myself that I was suddenly allergic to almonds – a food that I'd eaten almost daily for over a decade. I often woke up in the middle of the night with anxiety attacks and rarely got more than three or four hours of good sleep. I started separating myself from my family, not wanting them to get too close to me, somehow thinking that this would lessen the blow of an untimely death.

On the outside, life was still good.

Despite my growing quirks and struggles, I had a strong faith, a loving family, a great job as a University professor and administrator – I was becoming a nationally and internationally sought-after keynote speaker and consultant – and I had a growing list of accolades on my resume. I wasn't just sitting in a room with the lights off, depressed and unable to get out of bed, at least not most of the time.

Nonetheless, I lived in constant fear. I rarely went more than a half-day without fixating on images of death and fears of abandoning my family. I met with a psychologist a few times, and despite loving to tell me as often as possible that I reminded her of Sheldon from *Big Bang Theory*, she said that I didn't need her help. She told me I just needed to put things into perspective, stop exaggerating, and get on with life.

So, I did.

Some days went great. Other days felt like steps backward, and I wondered if those moments were what Simon and Garfunkel were talking about when they wrote the lyrics "Hello darkness my old friend."

There was no question that my life felt much more like "The Sound of Silence" than the "Sound of Music," but life was still incredibly good. I felt a confusing mix of being extremely blessed and hopelessly depressed.

Then, through a strange series of events, I discovered a treasure trove of insights and practices that changed my life perspective. I started reading about the incredible discoveries highlighted in a growing field referred to as positive psychology. Where traditional psychology often looked at helping people work through mental health challenges, the positive psychology literature looked at people who were flourishing in their lives, offering insights on promising perspectives and practices for well-being. The more I read, the more excited I became about the possibilities. Not only did I read about positive psychology, I developed a simple method for testing these practices in my own life.

It is one thing to read about new ideas, but it is a completely different one to put them into practice, keeping what works for you and setting aside what doesn't. I started referring to these as life experiments and quests. I researched and read about a promising practice. Then I assigned myself a life experiment, something that allowed me to test the practice for myself.

The more I experimented, the better I felt. Before long, I found myself experiencing more joy and contentment and the drive to take calculated risks, discover new things, and enjoy the many incredible gifts all around me.

The funny thing is that the practices were rarely based upon an incredible new scientific discovery. Most of the time, they were simple, commonsense practices. I could have read a thousand positive psychology books and never experienced this sort of transformation. The important part is that I was doing something and not just thinking about the ideas. The change came from my persistent commitment to acting, to learning by doing, and to engaging in simple life experiments.

Life isn't perfect today. I still have my down times. Fear and anxiety occasionally show up in my thoughts and actions more than I want. Sometimes those old fears get the best of me, but it is increasingly rare. Today my life is much fuller than it was a decade ago. I experience more joy and gratitude, a greater sense of adventure, stronger connections with people around me, and a willingness to lean into and learn from diverse people and novel experiences.

I'm less angry and more curious.

Life is full of wonder and awe-inspiring glimpses of grace.

But that's just the beginning.

Even though I'd already experienced modest professional successes, discovering this treasure took me to an entirely new level in my life's work. With this renewed energy and mindset, I found myself more effective at work, which led to new relationships and opportunities. My already growing consulting work reached a level where I had to decline the vast majority of the offers I received. I was so focused that I wrote, co-authored, and published seven books in less than four years. I earned a competitive fellowship at a prestigious college, leading me and my family on a splendid 6-month adventure to a new part of the country.

It isn't like all this magically appeared. Much of it grew out of years of work and developments, but what I discovered unquestionably put me in a position for greater achievements and an openness to embrace new opportunities.

By the way, I also started to fail at more things too, and I liked it. I took risks, learned from mistakes, and grew from them. Life became more of an adventure, and we all know that true adventures need challenges and difficulties, even some failures. Yet, with a deep sense of meaning and mission, these adventures are priceless.

This might sound too good to be true, and it is. I don't want to give an inauthentic view that I have it all together. I don't, and I don't even feel a need to have it all together. What I can say with confidence is that I've discovered that cultivating a more positive outlook and a deeper sense of meaning and purpose in life is achievable.

Not everyone can relate to the exact experiences that I just shared with you, but I know that countless people are grappling with fear, anxiety, negativity, stagnation, and other undesirable mental habits and emotional states. These are impacting their family life, friendships, work, and overall life satisfaction.

The Origin of The Twelve Quests

Several years ago, my son and daughter became interested in Greek and other mythologies. The more they read and talked about these incredible and time-tested stories, the more interested I became. Somehow, my childhood intrigue with these narratives re-surfaced.

One day I found myself re-reading a version of the *12 Labors of Hercules*. I first read this myth as a ten-year-old when I came across the book in my elementary school library. When each school day ended, I spent an hour or two in the library, along with other students, in a quasi-free form, afterschool program for children. There was the group that gathered and played Dungeons and Dragons. There were a few who rushed to get a seat at one of the available computers. A few studious types sat at tables and quietly completed their homework. I wandered from place to place, scanning the shelves and the art that seemed to change weekly. On this day, my wandering revealed a short book about the labors of Hercules. I read it and re-read it. For days, it was one of the only things that I thought about. Then I hid it away somewhere in the vault of my mind until I was in my early 40s, prompted to revisit this beloved tale because of my children's interest in the topic.

Around the same time that I revisited this classic myth, I was conducting research on the potential benefits of a newer and growing sub-field in psychology known as positive psychology. While some psychologists focus upon studying people struggling with mental health, I learned that positive psychologists sought to learn from people who were thriving, experiencing high levels of psychological and emotional well-being.

Why do some people flourish even in times of adversity? What is it that leads some people to be perpetual optimists, and is this something that can be learned by others? How is it that some people are frozen by fear, while others break through their fears, embracing them, and use these experiences to catapult themselves to new levels of accomplishment or well-being? How do some thrive when they encounter people who are different from them? How does grit and perseverance develop in a person, and what are its benefits?

These are the intriguing questions that positive psychologists study, and I became fascinated to find out what this research could do for me personally and what it could do to support more hopeful and self-empowering people, workplaces, and learning communities. As an educator and University administrator, most of what I study serves this dual purpose – personal growth and seeking ways to champion promising models and practices – in education.

I read the *12 Labors of Hercules*, but I had all this positive psychology research in the back of my mind at the same time. That combination led me on a series of experiences that expanded my heart and mind in unexpected but delightful ways.

Reading about Hercules' labors, I found myself craving some adventures of my own. Not that I wanted to take on the Hound of Hell or do anything that put my life in danger, but I craved more adventure in my life. My work at the time was meaningful, but it was beginning to feel mundane, and I was less inspired than a few years before.

Yet as I already mentioned, I was also experiencing an existential moment prompted by the birth of my son, and I was looking for more. I craved a greater sense of adventure and hated how I let fear and anxiety limit my choices and options in life. I wanted to go on some quests, be stretched and challenged, and hopefully return home having successfully completed the quest, having grown as a person in a meaningful way.

That is when the idea came to me.

What if I played both the role of King Eurystheus and Hercules? As the king, I would be responsible for coming up with a series of quests or challenges. Unlike the original quests, focused upon a blend of cunning and physical prowess, these quests would be about expanding my mind, deepening my sense of meaning and connection with others. I could use my developing knowledge of positive psychology to send myself on gratitude quests and fear-conquering quests. Playing the role of Hercules, I would accept each new quest, strive to accomplish the task before me, and embrace the opportunity to expand my heart and mind along the way.

So, I did it. I started with simple challenges around being more grateful. Then I explored quests around experiencing more wonder in life. I added quests about overcoming fears. Over the course of nearly three years, I experimented and played with more than 50 simple, practical, but challenging quests that helped me move from reading and knowing about the psychology of well-being to experiencing more of it in my life.

Some of the quests didn't work out as I expected, and I failed at quite a few of them as well. I often turned back to the positive psychology research to discover new ways to frame a quest. Then I ventured into well-known but ancient sources of wisdom about many of these topics, looking for new ideas and possibilities to add some mystery, meaning, and richness to each quest.

It might sound extravagant, but this series of "life experiments" changed my life. I'm still the same person that I was before, but my life started feeling more vivid, like the difference between watching something on an old analog television and shifting to the latest in visual technology. You notice things that you didn't before.

The colors are more vibrant.

Somewhere along the line, I decided that it was time for me to invite others to go on some of these quests as well, so I wrote this book, and it represents 12 quests – going along with the *12 Labors of Hercules*. It is my sincere hope and prayer that the adventures fueled by this book will bless you with a deepening sense of meaning, that they will add a vividness to your life that gives you a greater measure of joy.

CHAPTER 1

PREPARING FOR YOUR QUESTS

Twelve Quests is a guidebook, a modern version of Hercules' Twelve Labors (also known as the dodecathlon). Each chapter is a one to four-week quest.

Instead of physical feats, these quests are mental, emotional, and experiential challenges focused on what both science and ancient wisdom identify as promising pathways to well-being.

This is not a religious text. It is not about health and wealth. This is not a book about new information as much as it is a guidebook, a treasure map that only has value if you accept each new quest and act. While a different path than Thoreau, this is an invitation to "live deep and suck out all the marrow of life." It is also a chance to play, explore, experiment, connect, and add a little more adventure to your life. It is an invitation to embrace your personal dodecathlon.

It contains simple but profound challenges to expand your heart and mind in new ways, but it will not happen by reading the book alone.

You will have to act.

The more quests you complete, the more life vistas you are likely to experience, some of which have the potential to add incredible richness, meaning, and depth to your life.

This is not another self-help book focused on giving you more head knowledge. This book is not about information. It is about you and what you want to do and become. It is an invitation to a series of adventures that offer a chance for greater well-being and personal fulfillment. This is about your personal dodecathlon, inspired by the first dodecathlon, more commonly known as the *12 Labors of Hercules*.

Amid the darkest moment in his life, young Hercules turned to the oracle of Delphi to learn how he could atone for his past. The oracle directed Hercules to serve King Eurystheus of Tyrins for 12 years. If completed successfully, he would be rewarded with immortality, and he would pay for his past mistakes.

Accepting the oracle's guidance, Hercules offered himself in service to the king, not knowing what he would be commanded to do. The king happily accepted Hercules' offer and gave him his first task. But it was not an ordinary task, something that a typical soldier or servant would handle.

King Eurystheus knew of Hercules and his strength, so he sent the demigod into situations that would even push the limits of a young man with the blood of the gods running through his veins.

Over the next 12 years, Hercules accepted each new quest, overcame seemingly impossible odds but returned each time having accomplished the task set before him. He slayed the Nemean Lion, the nine-headed Hydra, and the Stymphalian Birds. He stole the Mares of Diomedes, the girdle of the great Queen of the Amazons, the cattle of Geryon, and the apples belonging to the Nymphs of the West. He cleaned the Augean stables in a single day. He captured the Golden Hind, the Erymanthian Boar, the Cretan Bull, and the Hound of Hades. Through these quests, he was able to atone for his mistakes and achieve immortality.

The quests in this book do not require the strength or cunning of a demigod or place you in the physical dangers associated with capturing the Hound of Hades. Nor do they offer you the promise of immortal life. They are quests that demand and reward resolve, risk-taking, and inner strength. Not only do they reward these traits, they help you build them. By accepting and persisting with each new quest, you are putting yourself in positions where these and many other capacities will grow. You are infusing your life with deep, meaning-rich experiences.

In terms of immortal life, that is beyond the scope of this book. As I already explained, this is not a religious book. While I am a deeply religious person and my own Christian faith certainly informs how I think and frame some of the ideas in this book, this is not an explicitly Christian book. In fact, many of the themes and ideas appear in many faith traditions and are embraced by those who do not affiliate with any particular religious doctrine. At the same time, when I began experimenting with these practices in my life, I found them affirming and deepening my own beliefs and values.

Some might argue that the fruit of these labors offer nutrients that can lengthen life, but my primary concern is to invite you on an adventure that can deepen your life and offer you ways to fill your life with rich and inspiring temporal meaning. I hope to provide you with experiences that develop ways of thinking and knowing that can expand your sense of connection in opportunities that you see in the world around you.

Maybe it is best that you not even think of this as an ordinary book. Instead, as I described it before, consider it part treasure map and part guidebook. Wandering the digital streets or browsing the great archives of your local library or bookstore, you came across a small text with the simplest of titles, "*12 Quests*." Drawn to the book by some undefined or unexplained desire, you opened it up to find a 12-part treasure map. The treasure at the end of the journey is not one of precious gems and gold, but it is something that can help you to see what is precious all around you and what is inside of you. Like King Midas, the treasure can give you a twist on the Midas touch, one that allows you to see the gold in even the most ordinary of events and circumstances in your life. This is a treasure of rich meaning and a new set of powers that you can use for years to come. These are not magical or super-powers like what we read in the great legends and myths. Instead, they are ways of thinking, knowing, and being that have transformed countless lives throughout history.

The Legacy of Quests

A quest is a particular type of adventure. The word itself comes from the Latin word for "question." It is an adventure with a purpose. It is one informed by a burning question, a mission-minded search, a driven pursuit of answers, a hunt for valued treasure. One of the most well-known quests in Western history is the Quest for the Holy Grail.

The Holy Grail was believed to be the cup of the Last Supper before the crucifixion of Jesus, later used to capture the blood that flowed from the side of Jesus when it was pierced on the cross. The purpose of ancient quests for the Holy Grail ranged from the pursuit of immortal life by drinking from the cup, to the belief that the cup offered healing to the people and land at the time. This great quest captured the intrigue of people throughout history, finding its way into 20th and 21st century novels, films, and popular culture.

Most intriguing in the retelling and rewriting of Holy Grail quests is that there are so often multiple layers of meaning in the search. It is rarely a straightforward hunt for a cup from where the seeker finds the grail, drinks, and is then granted immortality. Instead, the quest itself offers life-altering lessons and perspectives to the seekers, regardless of whether they find the cup. The growth and reward of the seekers of the grail doesn't come in the form of the grail. Instead, they are found in the journey.

The quests in this book, unlike the grail, have direct rewards, but that is only a portion of the benefit. As with the quest for the Holy Grail, the journey offers as many benefits and lessons as the destination.

You won't necessarily see the changes in yourself, at least not immediately. But others will notice, and over time, you will see them as well. Sometimes they are subtle adjustments in how you think and what occupies your thoughts. In other instances, they will be life-changing. You will find other benefits as well.

Since these quests build on each other, completing one quest will often give you skills useful in accomplishing the next. You will also find yourself prepared to start and finish other quests, those not described in this book, of your own making.

By the time you finish this book, you will find you can reframe your thinking about life into a series of quests. It will give you the opportunity to recognize the incredible wonder and adventure of life.

A Few Tips for Your Journeys

Before you get started, I want to offer you 10 travel tips. They come from direct experiences on my own quests, but are also drawn from literature across the ages, including newer findings about positive psychology. I invite you to experiment with these tips and make them your own. Some of them take time and practice to discover their real power, so beware of giving up on one too quickly. Use these tips as springboards into these quests; just remember that they are tips, not strict rules that need to be followed.

1. Find Your Mentors

While grand quests throughout history are sometimes lonely, even with times of isolation, they are never solitary. Behind and alongside every hero is a mentor, sometimes many mentors. As you embrace each new quest, look for your mentors. Seek them out.

You may find a mentor who will support you and offer you wisdom across multiple quests. You may even find a different mentor for each new quest. Consider a great hero's journey like the Star Wars Saga. Yes, Yoda served as a mentor for Luke. Though Luke knew a little bit about the force, like summoning small objects and avoiding lasers, Yoda took Luke's knowledge to a completely different level. But how many other mentors were there in his life, even at his earliest quests as a child?

Pick your favorite story of a hero or heroine. Any story will do.

Can you identify the mentors? Some are present at the very beginning of a story. Others appear later, or they come and go at opportune or unfortunate moments. Without these mentors, the heroes would have never succeeded.

Even though these are often characters in fictional stories, they point us to something very real about the quests in our own lives. We are all enriched by mentors.

In fact, it is fair to say that many great quests require mentors for one to succeed.

With the quests in this book, some might seem simple and straightforward, and you might be inclined to try them alone. While that confidence and independence will serve you well at times, you also need to embrace the value of mentors.

Seek them out.

For you, it might be as simple as a morning cup of coffee with a wise colleague. It might be someone who will teach you a new skill or offer sage advice for your journey. Keep your eyes and ears open, and you may be surprised what you can learn and from whom those lessons will come.

2. Embrace New Allies

Similarly, grand adventures are often team efforts. There is nothing requiring you to go through each of these quests on your own. Luke Skywalker didn't. He had Han Solo, Princess Leia, Chewie, R2-D2, C-3PO, Lando, Wedge, and the Ewoks. Some of these allies came from unexpected places. Some were good friends and family members. The same goes for you.

Invite and seek out others who might be inspired to join you on a quest. There is no question that there are family members, friends, colleagues, and maybe even co-workers who might need and want exactly what these quests have to offer. Sometimes this is about going on the journey side-by-side, sharing your lessons and encouraging one another.

In other situations, you might choose to each go on the quest alone, but in parallel. You can find time to meet and encourage one another, though you are each taking it on as a personal quest.

3. Be Prepared for Tests of Will (Doubts & Adversity)

Quests involve risk and uncertainty. There is no guarantee of success or that you will achieve your desired outcome. Embrace the risk and enjoy the mystery of life that unfolds as you live it. That is okay, because failure can be a gift as well.

Some quests are hard. They will challenge your resolve. You may find yourself distracted by something during your journey. This is good too. People grow by pushing themselves to their limits. Persevering through such challenges only contributes to your pride and sense of accomplishment at the end, even if you fall short.

Doubt is a likely companion on these quests as well. Sometimes, just as things get difficult, doubt will whisper in your ear, urging you to give up and recognize that you don't have what it takes, or it will try to convince you that the entire quest is not worth the time and effort. Some may tell you to silence or ignore the doubt.

I offer another option.

Welcome it as a companion, but do not let it lead the way or make the decisions. Sometimes we get important lessons from our doubts. They may force you to step back, re-evaluate the situation, and approach it differently. They might just be telling you to quit. But you can repurpose that message as a helpful guide to look for other ways forward.

Too many movies about quests and grand adventures mislead us. As the creators fit months or years of an adventure into a ninety-minute motion picture, we fail to feel and experience the depth of doubt – how it haunts the hero or heroine for hours, days, weeks, or even throughout the entire adventure.

In actual quests, the prevalence and significance of doubt and discouragement feels far more intense. And yet, persistence through such resistance is part of what sculpts our character, deepens our experience, and contributes to the pride and sense of accomplishment at key milestones and at the end of our journey.

4. Beware of Foes

Just as there are allies or friends, you will face foes. Maybe they are intentionally trying to undermine your efforts. More often, they are working through their own issues, and it expresses itself in hurtful or unhelpful ways. Recognize that foes are part of any quest but keep yourself focused on your mission.

Foes come in many forms. Some may question or mock the entire premise of these quests and life experiments. Some might genuinely believe that they are doing you a service by trying to set you straight, but there is usually something else at work, something you will not see or understand. It is not always clear what they hope to achieve.

While some of the great myths and quests of old involve conquering foes along the way, your goal won't be as gruesome. You'll want to show compassion and kindness but keep focused on what you are trying to accomplish. In other cases, maybe this is indeed a conflict that needs your time and attention. Only you will know what is best.

With that said, recognize that such challenges are part of the journey. They are to be expected, even if it is sometimes sad or disappointing to discover that they come from people and places that we didn't expect. We hoped to have their support and encouragement. In our mind, we might have even envisioned them as potential allies.

Whatever the case, remember that these encounters are an important and valuable part of your quest. They might even offer some of the most precious lessons and treasures. Listen, learn, show compassion, but also put it in the perspective of the entire quest.

5. Personalize the Time

These quests are designed in a way that you can pursue one over a week, a month, or even longer if you choose. It is up to you to determine the time that works best, but I strongly urge you to block out or schedule time for each quest and to give yourself a completion date. It can be tempting to set the goal of a longer time period, but if you have doubts about your ability to persevere amid the other demands on your time, choose something shorter, perhaps a week, for each quest.

Some might opt to have a few days or a week of rest between quests, while others may have the time and stamina to go directly from one to the next. Again, you know what works best for you and what your life and schedule will allow.

When I first completed the quests, I dedicated between a week and a month to each one, but most were seven to ten days. I found that to be just the right amount of time. I usually gave myself a couple days off, and then I ventured out on the next quest.

The important part is to choose and use time to help you get the most out of each adventure. Find what allows you to invest in each one, to pause and reflect, to learn, and to enjoy. If your schedule is turning the quest into a chore, consider shifting things around. These quests are not meant to be easy or constantly fun; they are intended to be rich, rewarding, and meaningful.

6. Consider a Secret Quest

Not all of your quests need to be obvious to those around you. Go through one or each of these quests in secret. A close friend or family member might know a little bit about what you are doing, but nothing explicit. For me, it worked well. It added to the mystery and sense of adventure.

7. Consider a Team Quest

On the other hand, this book is a great collection of team exercises. You can consider finding a friend, family member, colleague, or even a group of people who agree to go through the quests at the same time. This doesn't necessarily mean that you complete the quest as a team. It could be that you do it at the same time and pace, and you encourage or support one another. Maybe you create a dedicated Facebook group or other place to share stories, seek wise advice, encourage, and get encouraged. In this way, you are building a team of allies, creating a forum where you can help each other as you go on each new adventure.

This type of group approach is a great motivator for some people. Even if you love the idea of completing these quests, the discipline of follow-through can be a hindrance. That is where having a group can provide much needed accountability. Your persistence on each new quest is what keeps you connected to that group, and that is often an added motivation to keep going on those days when you feel like quitting.

8. Watch out for the Temptation to Quit Right Before the Treasure

The idea of quitting will occur to you at various times in your journey. You are pursuing these quests amid busyness and other demands of your life. These demands will shout for your attention, and you will have compelling reasons and excuses to stop. You might be faced with a justifiable reason to take a break, but don't be too quick to listen to your inner voice. Perseverance is necessary to achieve most great things in life, and that includes persisting through an array of emotions and mental states. Remember that they are temporary, and there are beautiful vistas ahead, moments that will inspire and motivate you well into the future.

9. *Recognize that Quitting is Sometimes Perfectly Appropriate*

There are all kinds of stories. Among them are comedies and tragedies. Comedies end with celebration and success. Tragedies do not. While we might be tempted to define one as good and the other as bad, that's not the case, especially as we think about each quest. Some quests do not turn out as we expect them to. We find that we reach a limit, and do not see a way around it.

That is okay. There may be circumstances in your life that demand greater attention.

This is for all of you type-A and goal-driven people who will do anything to complete what you start. It's a commendable trait in many situations, maybe even most, but there are times to give up.

There were experiments that I had to put on hold. I eventually returned to them, but amid the experiment, I found greater priorities emerge. In one case, I learned that I didn't have what it took to complete the quest, not at that moment.

These aren't meant to be excuses allowing you to give up because things get hard, or because you're afraid. Remember, this is a playful collection of quests meant to enrich your life, not a list of reasons to pile guilt on your shoulders.

10. Keep a Treasure Chest

I wish that someone offered me this advice before I started on my quests. So much of what I experienced is lost or forgotten because I didn't take time to collect and record the treasured lessons and moments throughout my journeys. I eventually learned to do this, but not at first. I'm talking about journaling, capturing pictures or videos, or maybe even blogging about your journey through each quest.

The quest itself is full of great moments, but I soon discovered that the planning in advance of the quest and the reflection after the fact sometimes offered as many, or more, lessons and positive moments as the quest itself. These lessons and moments will be enhanced if you make the decision – before you begin – to establish some sort of treasure chest where you record and store these things, a place you can continually return to enjoy what you discovered and experienced along the way.

It is Time to Begin

I offer these tips to help you amid what I hope you find to be a rich and rewarding journey. There is so much more that could be shared, but you will soon begin to develop your own list of tips, guidelines, and lessons learned and earned amid the joys and challenges of heeding the call and embarking on each new quest. You have everything that you need for this journey.

In many traditions, journeys are begun with a formal send off, a farewell until we meet again, a prayer, or a word of blessing. With this beautiful tradition in mind, I close this chapter with the following words:

"As you head out on these quests, may each new treasure leave you blessed. May your adventure be full of mystery and meaning, wonder and play. May truth, beauty, and goodness come to you each day. And may you have the eyes to see that all of these are merely glimpses of treasures in eternity."

CHAPTER 2

THE GRATITUDE QUEST

"He is a wise man who does not grieve for the things which he has not, but rejoices for those which he has."
-Epictetus

"Gratitude is the sign of noble souls."
-Aesop

At mealtime, A.J. Jacobs started a family tradition of thanking the many people who helped make the meal before him possible. He thanked the farmers that grew the food, and then he went all the way to the people at the grocery store. One day, Jacobs' son challenged him to take this a step further.

"Why don't you thank these people in person?" he asked.

This challenge launched Jacobs on a grand adventure around the world discovering, meeting, and thanking the many people who helped make his morning coffee a reality. Jacobs retells the full story in his book, *Thanks a Thousand.*

Think of the many people who not only make the world better, but make your life better, even if just in small ways like contributing to your morning cup of coffee. Take a moment to catalog all the items in your life that contribute to a positive start to your morning. You might begin with your bed; the sheets; your clothing; the end table; the books or other items beside your bed; your toothbrush and toothpaste; your shower and the water that finds its way into your house; the electricity that powers the lights; your morning coffee; whatever you eat for breakfast; the table where you sit for breakfast; or the yoga mat or other fitness items.

Without going more than an hour into your morning, you can easily create a list of well over a hundred such items. How much do you know about how these things found their way into your home and life? What do you know about the people who contributed to the creation and delivery of these items?

Simply listing the items in your life, it doesn't take long to recognize the thousands or hundreds of thousands of people who contributed to what you use and value in your daily life. Their contribution and work, even if seemingly small, enriches your life. It's easy to see that we are connected to far more people than many of us ever pause to consider. Reflecting on this reality is enough to evoke wonder and gratitude – wonder at the incredible complexity and connectedness in our world and gratitude for the nameless people with whom you are connected, even if just by a tube of toothpaste.

Your first quest is an opportunity to explore this reality, to experience the wonder and gratitude that comes from seeing the world in this way. This is a chance to learn, to experience more gratitude, to connect with others, and to cultivate an ongoing sense of gratitude that is likely to stay with you long after you finish the quest. It is not a simple challenge in that it requires your time, commitment, and effort.

This quest will help create the conditions for you to experience the joy that comes from showing gratitude, connecting with new people, learning more about those who contribute to meaningful things in your life, and sharing kind words with others.

The Quest

1. Begin by making a list of at least 20 things that give you joy or enrich your life in some way. For the sake of this experiment, focus on artifacts, systems, and experiences. Your list might look something like this: doing yoga in the morning; my first cup of coffee each day; going on an evening run; listening to the What is in the Air? podcast on the drive to work; hiking my favorite nearby trail; reading a great book on a rainy day; watching my favorite TV show; or hanging out with friends at the local pub each Friday.

2. Looking at your list, commit to learning about one or more key people who are responsible for making each of these items possible. If you have a favorite morning coffee, find out which company makes it, and who are the key people who helped make that company a reality. Who are the people that keep it running today? For the nearby trail, discover who maintains it or who helped make it a reality in the first place. You get the idea. Part of the fun in this project is researching the specific people who contribute to what you value in your life. Take your time, but continue until you identify one or more key people behind at least seven of the items on your

list.

3. Next, block off seven consecutive days on your calendar, assigning one of the seven items (and the associated person) to each day.

4. For each of these seven days, your task is to locate an email address or contact information, and write a brief but considerate thank you letter to that person. Obviously, traveling to people and thanking them in person could be a grand adventure indeed, but for this experiment, you might want to just start with a letter.

5. Be sure to send the email or letter by the end of each day.

6. At the end of the week, or maybe even during the week, set aside time to journal and reflect upon the experiment. What did you learn? Did this experiment impact your mood or outlook? How did this experiment increase your awareness of the countless people who contribute to that which you value? Are there any lessons or practices that you might want to continue even after this experiment is over?

Tips for the Journey

- Doing the work of finding contact information in advance of your seven-day challenge might help you stay on track. Sometimes this will require a bit of detective work.

- While you can certainly find and contact the primary source for some things, like the musician who wrote or performed that song that means so much to you, you can also think about some of the other people who contributed to the song making its way to you. In other words, sometimes you might want to thank the key figure or celebrity, but it can be just as meaningful (maybe even more so) to contact the others who get far less recognition.

- This is an experiment about three different things. First, you are cultivating thoughts of gratitude. Second, you are putting faces and names to the things in your life, finding delight in discovering the many people who contribute to what you value. Third, you are connecting with others and sharing kind words. Our world can always use more kindness, and by taking on this challenge, you are making that happen. Thank you.

"Gratitude bestows reverence, allowing us to encounter everyday epiphanies, those transcendent moments of awe that change forever how we experience life and the world."
-John Milton

CHAPTER 3

THE SAVORING AND SHARING QUEST

"You can't let one bad moment spoil a bunch of good ones."
-Dale Earnhardt

"Savor the moment." You've probably received that advice at some point in your life. It is an invitation to hold on to a moment that is good, to recognize that it is precious, and to give it your attention. The Online Cambridge Dictionary offers this definition of savoring: "To enjoy food or an experience slowly, in order to appreciate it as much as possible." We can savor memories, present moments, plans for the future, and even creative moments that never make it beyond our imagination.

Fred Bryant is sometimes referred to as the father of the psychology of savoring, being among the first to research and publish on the nature of savoring and its potential benefits. While and older book today, *Savoring: A New Model of Positive Experience* remains a seminal work, one rich with relevant insights. Stemming from Bryant's initial work, today we have a growing body of literature on the subject, research that points us to the positive benefits of savoring in our lives.

While there are many simple life experiments that you can conduct to explore the benefits of savoring in your own life, one of the easiest and most accessible is to begin with an exercise focused on savoring past moments. With that in mind, the following is a straightforward, seven-day experiment to get you started. It was inspired by literature about the psychology of savoring past moments combined with literature about the benefits of storytelling and connecting with others. In other words, this is not only about savoring; it is about sharing your savoring with others. Since positive emotion spreads, why not share this with others?

The Quest

1. The best way to follow through on an experiment is to commit to it upfront and schedule it. As a result, block off 10 minutes on your calendar for seven consecutive days.

2. Before day 1, make a list of your top 10 to 20 most positive memories. They could be about anything, but for the sake of this experiment, choose ones that you are comfortable sharing with other people. You will not use all of these, but the list will prime your thinking for each of your seven 10-minute savoring activities in the upcoming days.

3. On the first day, when you reach your scheduled 10-minute appointment, choose one of the items from the pre-developed list and start writing about what you remember. Record and remember

as many sensory elements as possible. What did it look like, smell like, sound like, feel like…? Write about the positive emotions that you remember. What did you feel? Next, think about putting how this happened into writing. What led to this event? Who contributed to it? What role did you play in making it happen? This doesn't need to be long, but you should try to keep writing for five to ten minutes.

4. Read through what you wrote at least twice, making any relevant updates or edits.

5. Next, share what you wrote with at least one other person; or, if you want, you can turn this into a social media sharing exercise. Just make sure that it is something you are comfortable sharing with whatever audience has access to your social media post.

6. Repeat this each day for the next seven days.

7. About halfway through the experiment, and at the end, take time to write and reflect about what you are learning from the experiment. Do you notice anything from it? How do others respond when you share these memories?

Tips for the Journey

• Don't worry about the quality of your writing. You can make this a bullet list; just try to be as vivid and detailed as possible. This will help you savor the memory.

- When it comes to sharing your memory, choose what you are comfortable with. It might be sharing with a friend or family member, someone who agrees to do the experiment at the same time as you; or you can go the social media route. Think about the audience, taking into consideration what you are comfortable sharing and what you prefer to keep to yourself.

- Sometimes you will be tempted to depress positive emotions or engage in what psychologists call dampening. You might be tempted to minimize the memory, excuse or dismiss it, avoid fully experiencing the positive emotion, or use other mechanisms to downplay or diminish it. This is why writing is an important part of this experiment. It will help you resist those negative thoughts. What you write should focus only on the positive experience and memory.

"Life is all memory, except for the one present moment that goes by you so quickly you hardly catch it going."
-Tennessee Williams

Chapter 4

THE CHILD'S PLAY QUEST

"A person's maturity consists in having found again the seriousness one had as a child, at play."
-Friedrich Nietzsche

Play is often defined as purposeless, an activity for enjoyment, recreation, or entertainment. When I looked up synonyms for play, I came across words like frolic, romp, and cavort. Perhaps this is why some people find play unbecoming of an adult.

These people are missing out.

There is so much research showing that play is an important part of becoming a functioning adult, as it is important for an adult to retain a healthy measure of inner child.

Play is also something that transcends time and culture. Play, playfulness, and games of different types are present in every culture in the world, and this is true as far back as we can study human civilization.

Play is a universal language.

The games might be different, but even if you don't speak the language or understand the culture, there are simple games and forms of play that remain a means of connecting with other people. There are games, even today, that are shared across cultures. Whether you grew up in Brazil, Belgium, Rwanda, or the United States, take out a soccer ball and you have a means of connecting with others in a meaningful way.

While there are many types of play, some structured and others unstructured, this experiment is focused on a structured form of play that we know as a game. Jane McGonigal, in *Reality is Broken,* offers a simple definition of a game: a game can be anything that includes a goal, rules, a feedback system (Am I getting closer to the goal?), and voluntary participation (fun). This can include everything from video games to board games and card games.

Play is good for the mind, body, and soul, and this life experiment is a chance to experiment with adding a little more play to your life.

The Quest

1. This challenge is a simple one. You are going to play one game a day for seven days in a row. It can be any type of game that you choose, but to keep things interesting, you only have eight different types for this challenge. Choose seven of them: (1) a card game, (2) a strategy game, (3) a board game, (4) a multi-player video game, (5) a guessing game, (6) a word game, (7) a conversation game, and (8) a game that you make up. (See the 4 simple rules above.)

2. First, review your calendar and choose seven consecutive days for this challenge.

3. Next, using the links and explanations of the

different types of games provided here (or you can draw from your own resources), pick a game for each category that you have never played, or that you have not played for at least 10 years.

4. Now that you've selected your games, you can either assign a game to each day on your calendar, or you can randomly choose one of the games each day.

5. Make time to reflect and journal about your thoughts and experiences throughout the week, giving some extra time at the end.

Tips for the Journey

- Have fun!

- Consider blocking off a certain time each day to play the game; or maybe you want to enjoy seeking out and creating time more spontaneously. Either way, you don't go to bed at night without playing one of the games you've selected.

- These games don't need to be long. If you are tight for time, limit yourself to 15 or 30 minutes a day for the game. Just choose games where that will work.

- If you don't play video games, consider asking a friend or family member to be your tour guide. The same can go for any of these categories.

- Involve others in the fun. You might ask one or more person to join you in the challenge, either playing the games together, or just doing this at the same time and sharing your stories and experiences.

- For the day where you make up the game, it doesn't need to be elaborate. Keep it simple. Keep it fun.

CHAPTER 5

THE CONNECTIONS QUEST

"You can make more friends in two months by becoming interested in other people than you can in two years by trying to get other people interested in you."
-Dale Carnegie

One of the first professional books that I read after graduating from college was a text by Dr. Howard Gardner called *Frames of Mind*. This is the book that popularized the concept of multiple intelligences, the theory that people are not defined by a single IQ or intelligence quotient. It's actually more accurate to recognize that we each have multiple intelligences: musical, visual-spatial, verbal-linguistic, logical-mathematical, bodily kinesthetic, interpersonal, intrapersonal, and naturalistic (added later). This is a theory that gained traction and attention in the 1990s and persists today.

It is an intriguing and important theory and a personally influential book. This book also represents a first experience for me. It was the first time I ever reached out to the author of a book I was reading.

In 1994, I'd only had an email address for a couple of years, and I was just beginning to discover the power, possibility, and connectivity of the Internet. While reading *Frames of Mind*, I highlighted ideas that intrigued me and wrote questions and notes in the margins. One day while I was reading the book and grappling to understand a part of it, a simple notion occurred to me for the first time in my life. I wondered if I could ask Howard Gardner a question about his book via email.

I moved over to my computer, searched for him by name, and located his profile as a faculty member on the Harvard University website. His email was readily available, so I copied it, pasted it into a new email message, crafted a few comments and my question, and sent it off. It felt like putting a message in a bottle and throwing it into the sea.

Was there any chance that he would reply?

He did, via an assistant, within two days! In that instant, reading a book turned into a two-way conversation with the author. I felt this sense of pride and accomplishment. I was honored to be acknowledged and deemed worthy of a response. Not only that, the author of every book after this became more real and accessible to me. I imagined each author at a desk, writing, thinking, and maybe pausing to address an email message from a reader like me.

When I started creating life experiments for myself years later, I recalled this early experience and the positive emotion that it created. I decided to turn it into a formal experiment. Below is not the exact one that I used, but it is close, and I encourage you to give it a try.

The Quest

1. Create a list of at least seven interesting things that you've read lately or hope to read in the future. For the sake of this experiment, pick short books, articles, essays, or something that will not take you days or weeks to read. Also, in preparation, find the email address or contact information for the author of each text that you select.

2. Now block off time on your calendar to read each of the articles or items – one each day.

3. On day one of the experiment, read the first item in your list, highlighting interesting ideas and recording questions or thoughts that come to mind as you read. Imagine that you will be going to coffee with the author in a couple hours. You want to be well-prepared. Read with curiosity.

4. Once you are finished reading, send a message to the author, expressing thanks for what they wrote, and then engage the author with a question or comment. Keep it short, sincere, and civil.

5. Repeat this each day for seven days.

6. At the end, take time to reflect on the experience. How many people replied to you? What did you think and feel? How did this experiment influence how you think about reading, how you think about writing? What's next?

Tips for the Journey

- Perhaps this should go without saying, but don't argue with the author. This is an experiment about connecting with people in a new way. You don't have to agree with what the author wrote, but you can use this as a chance to learn and understand a different perspective. This is not about winning a debate or sounding right. It is about connecting, listening, and learning.

- Don't take it personally if you never hear from the person, or if it is a short and underwhelming reply. People are busy, and some get lots of emails. You will likely get follow up from some assistants or others, depending upon the person.

- Keep in mind that you have no existing relationship with this person, so choose a tone, content, and a writing style that is appropriate.

- Speaking as an author of seven books, I love to hear from readers. While this might feel like you are imposing, you are not. You are being human and trying to connect.

- Consider what you can learn from this experiment. Personally, this experiment opened me up to reaching out to people far more often, and I can't begin to share the myriad of stories about where this led: new relationships; new insights; a sense of gratitude and satisfaction; a humanizing and personalizing of the author; job offers; and even trips to other parts of the country in some cases. Apart from all of that, it continues to ground me in this beautiful reality of meaningful connections with different people in the digital age.

CHAPTER 6

THE WONDER QUEST

"The world will never starve for want of wonders, but for want of wonder."
-G. K. Chesterton

"It's almost impossible to watch a sunset and not dream."
-Bernard Williams

How often do you experience wonder in your life, that sometimes indescribable blend of surprise and admiration? It could be a subtle movement of an infant, a beautiful sight in nature, being witness to an incredible physical achievement at an athletic event, or a moment of enchantment with an awe-inspiring poem or plot twist in a film or novel. Wonder is one of the most powerful but under-valued aspects of the human experience. Consider the fact that you can have a 15-second experience of wonder, and still be able to describe it with striking detail 20 years later.

Wonder is powerful, and it is good for you. There is a growing body of research to show an impressive list of benefits. Moments of wonder can increase your sense of well-being, cultivate humility, and increase your openness to people who are different from you. Sharing a moment of wonder with others can even create or strengthen a positive bond.

One readily accessible experience of wonder is witnessing a sunrise or a sunset. As such, this is a perfect starting point for experimenting with adding more wonder to your life. Depending upon the weather, these moments of wonder are available to you every morning and evening.

A team at Northwestern University looked at the connection between our sleep and early morning light. Another team at the same University identified a connection between morning light and reduced body mass index. As these and other studies indicate, enjoying nature at sunset and/or sunrise appears to have a favorable impact upon the circadian rhythms that regulate our sleeping patterns.

"Get outside. Watch the sunrise. Watch the sunset. How does that make you feel? Does it make you feel big or tiny? Because there's something good about feeling both."
-Amy Grant

Could it be that an activity as simple as enjoying a daily sunset or sunrise could improve your personal sense of well-being, improve your emotional state, help you sleep better, and maybe even help shed a few pounds? Why not try this life experiment and see for yourself?

The Quest

1. Find the sunset and sunrise times for the five to ten days.

2. Choose five days to watch sunrises and five days to watch sunsets, and schedule them in your calendar.

3. Most sunrises and sunsets take three to six minutes, but you will want to block off 10-15 minutes to enjoy them and then include a little time for quiet and reflection.

4. Consider setting an alarm five to ten minutes beforehand, or however long it will take you to get ready and in position.

5. Choose your spot in advance, get there on time, just sit (or stand), and enjoy. Enjoy the moment, the broader environment, and what sometimes seems like a magical time of day.

6. Consider bringing a journal to record any thoughts or reflections during or afterward.

7. At the end of the experiment, once you've enjoyed five sunrises and five sunsets, consider setting aside 20-30 minutes to reflect. Record your thoughts and observations. How were sunsets and sunrises different? Did you notice any changes for yourself during the experiment? How did this impact your sleep, your sense of well-being, or other parts of your life?

Tips for the Journey

- Is it safe to watch a sunrise and sunset? In general, experts seem to agree that staring at the sun is not safe, and that is not what I am suggesting here. There are health concerns about what is called "sun gazing" at sunrise, sunset, or at any point during the day. While you might find mixed views about the safety of looking directly at the sun during sunset and sunrise, there is no need to stare directly at the sun to enjoy this time and the benefits. Consider exploring the colors in the clouds, the surrounding sky, and the rest of the environment during these special times of day.

- Depending upon where you live or where you are for your sunrise/sunset experiments, there might obviously be a few clouds in the way. No worries. Check the weather in advance, and if weather is a problem, schedule a make-up day.

- You might want to experiment with doing this alone and with one or more people.

- If you have the time, consider experimenting with different locations, obviously planning your travel time so that you don't miss the big event.

- Did you experience some positive benefits? Consider scheduling a little time for sunrises and sunsets in the future, maybe even inviting others to join you on occasion.

- Beware of just turning each sunrise/sunset into a photo opportunity. If you want to capture and share the moment, take your picture, but then set the camera/phone aside to be fully present and enjoy the moment.

CHAPTER 7

THE REUNION QUEST

"The pain of parting is nothing to the joy of meeting again."
-Charles Dickens

"When the roots are deep there is no reason to fear the wind."
-African Proverb

Much of your life is a long series of connections and relationships with other people. Some of those connections persist today, while others come and go. Either way, each person with whom we interact is a part of our life story, like we are part of theirs. Even the most solitary and self-sufficient among us are indebted to dozens, hundreds, even thousands of people over the course of our lives.

How much do you think about the people from your past?

Every so often, we find ourselves reconnecting with past friends, colleagues, classmates, and distant family members. Maybe we encounter them in the airport, while out at a restaurant, at a conference, or at some unexpected place.

Perhaps we connect amid some of those milestone moments in life. We attend the wedding of a longtime friend, go to a high school reunion, our find ourselves at a funeral – seeing people whom we've not thought about for years, even decades.

In such moments, we might experience any number of thoughts and emotions. Maybe the awkwardness of the situation prompts us to hide or avoid the person, pretending we don't recognize them. Maybe we are drawn to such moments, and we are quick to take initiative to greet them with a few words or even a hug. Such chance re-connections can be moments of joy, anxiety, curiosity, or maybe even fear. Regardless, they draw us back into our past. Even a brief encounter can be enough to prompt hours or days of remembering and reliving, even learning about ourselves, where we've come from, where we are now, and where we hope to be in the future.

> *"I am a part of all that I have met."*
> *– Lord Tennyson*

Whether you are an extrovert who is energized by time around others, or you are an introvert who requires personal time for that same energy, all people crave and benefit from rich and meaningful human connections. We are designed that way, and even though we might initially dread the work or anxiety associated with meeting a new person or connecting with someone from our past, this effort attaches us to a deep, ancient, and persistent human need and craving.

This life experiment is one of several opportunities to experience and explore this reality for yourself. It is not easy, and the outcome is uncertain, but it taps into any number of our most fundamental yearnings. It offers a sense of adventure and mystery, provides the possibility for new forms of gratitude, and most fundamentally, it gives us a mirror for our own growth and allows us a chance to feed that yearning for human connection.

The Quest

1. This is designed as a four-week experiment but adapt it to meet your needs.

2. The first week of this quest is one of reflecting and remembering. Make a list of at least 20 people from your past that you have not seen or spoken to for at least five years. Depending upon your age, maybe you want to make that at least 10, 15, or 20 years in your past. You decide. Choose people who bring up fond memories for this experiment, but don't just rely on your memory. Check with friends and family members. Look at old yearbooks or photos. Browse your emails and work-related projects that might be sitting on your computer. As you make your list, use this as a chance to reminisce. Enjoy it.

3. If week one was about remembering and reminiscing, week two is your research and planning week. Choose at least four of the people from your list and find out where they are today. This quest calls for you to reconnect with at least four people from your initial list, one in each of the following ways, though you don't have to do

all the following during week two. Your only task this week is to do the preparation. That means finding contact information, choosing the people, etc.

4. Choose and plan for one person whom you can reach out to via email, simply explaining that their name came up for you recently and that you are wondering how they are doing. Sharing something for which you are grateful is always a good thing to include as well. You can also share a bit about yourself, but if things are going particularly well for you, be cautious about what might seem like boasting.

5. Choose and plan for a second person. For this one, you will do the same thing, but send the message the old-fashioned way, with a card or handwritten letter.

6. Now identify and plan for connecting with a third person, only for this one, you have the challenge of making a phone call.

7. Finally, for the fourth, you are going to plan for reaching out to the person and inviting that person to join you for coffee or lunch, just to connect.

8. Now, for weeks three and four, you have the quest of following through on each of your plans. Reach out, and if one doesn't work out, go back to your list and choose someone else.

Tips for the Journey

- Don't worry if some of these do not work out. That is why you are starting with a list of 20 people.

- This experiment can bring about a myriad of emotions. It is great to have a confidant, a friend or family member, so that you can talk through and debrief the experiences.

- Try to avoid the trap of comparisons. This is not about finding out whose life is the best. It is about connecting with people who are a valued part of your life story. Focus on gratitude, catching up on each other's lives, re-connecting, listening, and learning.

- While you might be tempted to use this experiment to mend broken relationships, and that is certainly your choice, this experiment is designed to connect around positive people and memories in your past. So, if you are craving to reconcile, consider leaving the mending of broken relationships for some future time, maybe even a future quest of your own design.

- As with all life experiments, I can't emphasize enough the value of reflection and journaling. What did you learn about yourself? What did you find yourself thinking and feeling? Might one of these connections turn into a rekindled friendship?

- These are positive people from your past, but don't forget about safety. Be wise and thoughtful about what you share and how you connect, just as you do with new friendships. It takes time to build trust, and that applies to people from your past as well.

- In an age of social media, it can be easy to "spy" on people from your past, but not actually reconnect with them. This is a quest to go beyond that, where you actually reach out.

CHAPTER 8

THE GIVING QUEST

"I am a little pencil in the hand of a writing God who is sending a love letter to the world."
-Mother Teresa

"No act of kindness, no matter how small, is ever wasted."
-Aesop

Too often, the habit of giving today has become transactional and commercial. Holidays like Christmas have turned into times of stress and consternation as much as joy. In 2018, there were reports that the holiday season exceeded one trillion dollars in sales. That is more than a fourth of all the healthcare expenses in the United States in a given year. It is also 10 times more than what is spent on college tuition in the United States annually. People have managed to turn giving into big business. Add to that the amount spent on gifts for birthdays, anniversaries, and other celebrations, and we are looking at a multi-trillion-dollar aspect of American life.

For all its commercialism, the willingness to spend so much on giving and celebrating points us to something extraordinary and fundamental about the human experience. We thrive upon and crave both celebrations and the act of giving. Giving is good for the soul and even for your physical well-being. The list of claims supported by emerging research about the physical and psychological benefits of giving are so grand as to evoke some suspicion: decreased blood pressure, lower stress levels, decreased depression, and the release of chemicals in the brain that generate happiness. One study, focused upon giving of one's time in the form of volunteerism, even suggested evidence that generosity might just lengthen a person's life.

It doesn't need to be an official holiday or a special event for gifts, and there is a growing body of research about the many benefits of giving – benefits for you, the recipient, and even those who witness the act of giving. Acts of kindness, including those in the form of gift giving, reduce stress and anger, boost the immune system, and combat anxiety and depression. It also just feels good to do something kind for another person. Kindness is one of those traits that transcends time and place, celebrated in every major world religion and culture.

For those who celebrate Christmas, some engage in a seasonal activity known as "Secret Santa." People draw a name from a hat and, over a few days or weeks leading up to Christmas, surprise a designated person with a gift. They do so without the recipient knowing the name of the giver. This life experiment is inspired by that tradition, but you don't need to wait for a certain time of year or special occasion.

You can start today.

The Quest

1. This is a four-week experiment, but as with all the others, adjust and adapt as you see fit. This is not about following a perfectly prescribed set of steps. These steps are just simple guidelines to get you started.

2. Starting today or at the beginning of the week, devote the first two days of the week identifying a person you want to surprise with a small-but-thoughtful gift. Your only task in day one and two is to choose the person. It can be a friend, family member, co-worker, or even a stranger.

3. For days three and four, observe, listen, and learn about this person with the goal of thinking up a gift that you are confident will help, encourage, or delight him or her.

4. On days five and six, make, purchase, and wrap the gift.

5. Finally, on day seven, secretly make the delivery.

6. At the end of each week, reflect on the process. What did you learn about the other person? What did you learn about yourself? How did this experiment influence your mood, thoughts, and emotions? Might you want to turn this into an ongoing habit, perhaps something that you do on a schedule during certain times of the year, once every month or two, or even some other timeline that makes sense to you? Maybe this experiment gives you ideas on how to make giving a more

common and frequent part of your life.

7. Repeat this for a different person in weeks two, three, and four.

Tips for the Journey

- While this experiment is designed to be done with one new person each week for four weeks, feel free to do it as few or as many times as you like. Perhaps you only want to commit to doing it for a single person, or maybe you want to extend it over an entire season or year.

- Enjoy the process of selecting the person and getting to know the person's needs and interests.

- The size of the gift doesn't matter. You might even want to limit yourself to a specific dollar amount.

- Have fun and be playful about how you package and deliver the gift. If that isn't possible, select and order a gift online and have it delivered to them. It could be as simple as a small gift card with an encouraging message.

- While you can select whomever you want, consider using this experiment to offer kindness to new people in your life or people beyond your regular network or community.

- Have fun. Don't overthink it.

- Don't forget to take the time to reflect and journal about your experience each week and perhaps for a little longer at the end of the experiment.

CHAPTER 9

THE HELPER QUEST

"When I was a boy and I would see scary things in the news, my mother would say to me, 'Look for the helpers. You will always find people who are helping.'"
-Fred Rogers

"Look for the helpers." While I never met him in person, Fred Rogers is one of the most significant mentors in my life. He is also arguably one of the greatest social entrepreneurs of the 20th century. His books, interviews, and episodes of *Mr. Rogers Neighborhood* are treasure troves of wise and memorable messages.

While we don't know much about Fred's childhood, there are moments that give us a glimpse, a hint, that this wisdom flowed through his family line like a secret and ancient royal bloodline. When considering the terrible things in the news, Fred recalled a piece of wisdom shared by his mother. When you see evil at work in the world, when you learn about tragedies and disasters, it is easy to focus on all that is going wrong. Yet, the wisdom shared by Fred's mother was this, "Look for the helpers." Look into the tragedy and, amid the grief and darkness, you will see bearers of courage, light, and hope. These are the helpers, the people who are moved to step up and step into these situations. They are the firefighters who rush back into a burning home to save one more life. They are the neighbors who band together to support and save one another amid a natural disaster. They are mothers, fathers, sons, daughters, emergency response team members, health care workers, and the unknown and un-named people who come to help even as others are running for safety.

We don't want to ignore the evil or diminish the grief by disregarding it. The helpers stand alongside the grieving. They see the evil so clearly that they are compelled to act, often putting others above themselves. They are, to some people, the heroes, and while our study of history often reveals that even the most revered people in our history are full of flaws and imperfections, we can still be inspired by the helpers in our world. As we look and learn from these helpers, we may even find ourselves conjuring the course and character to step up, speak up, reach out, lift up, and help. Our communities are better when we see, celebrate, ponder, and learn from the helpers, and this quest is an opportunity to do just that. This is an invitation to look for the helpers.

The Quest

1. This might seem like the opposite of the quest, but your first step is to search the news and headlines for 10 recent tragedies or troubling events. You might want to choose events that have been covered well by the media to make the rest of the quest easier. However, you may also want to pick a theme for your quest – a collection of events that relate to something that is particularly important to you. You might want to

select events that have been especially troubling to you over the years, allowing you to potentially reframe or expand your thinking about these events. All you need to do at this stage is to select the events and maybe gather links to two or three news articles about them. You don't even need to read them yet.

2. Pull out your calendar and block off at least 30 to 60 minutes each day for 10 consecutive days. If possible, it is best to choose a specific time, one that fits the rest of your life schedule, so that you are not inclined to skip it.

3. Now you are ready to get started. On each of the scheduled days and times that you block off, your challenge is to read the articles that you pre-select and do exactly what Fred Rogers' mother suggested. Look in those stories and beyond to find one or more helper. Where are the people who stepped up and helped? Who are they? What can you learn from them? Within the allotted time each day, your focus should be upon learning and thinking about one or more of the helpers with the first event in your list.

4. Within the next 24 hours, your challenge is to share the story of one or more of these helpers with someone else. You can share it with a friend or family member. If appropriate, you can share it with a colleague at work. You can also turn this into an act of public sharing, expressing what you are doing and thinking about, on your favorite social media outlet.

5. At least three or four times during the 10 days, set aside time to engage in some written reflection about your experience with this experiment. What are you seeing and learning? What are you noticing that you didn't notice before? How is this contributing to your thoughts about these and other tragedies? Do you notice any changes in your own thoughts, feelings, or sense of well-being?

Tips for the Journey

- Think twice before deciding to skip the sharing part of this challenge. Learning about the helpers and then telling others about the helpers are both important parts of deepening your own thoughts and reflections. I know that this might stretch you a little bit, and that is fine. If it feels like too much of a stretch, pick a close friend and ask that person in advance if they are willing to give you a few minutes each day to share what you are learning. It could even just be a short email, text, phone call, or video chat.

- If you are not ready to share, then consider pretend sharing. In other words, write an email or letter to someone about what you learned that day. You can throw it away or just send it to yourself, but challenge yourself to go through the act of telling the story of the helper.

- If you want to extend your sharing, this is a prime

opportunity to experiment with creating short videos on your phone and sharing them with others. You can do this with Facebook, YouTube, and any number of other simple technologies and tools. Then you can create and share a two to three-minute informal video of what you learned each day of this experiment.

- As always, I'm compelled to remind you that writing is a powerful reflective tool. Even if journaling is not "your thing," I invite you to consider it, even if just for this or a few of the experiments. The other benefit is that you can look back on your thinking weeks, months, or even years later; and it can be incredibly enlightening (or sometimes a little entertaining).

CHAPTER 10

THE HUMANIZATION QUEST

"I disagree with you but I'm pretty sure you're not Hitler."
-John Stewart

"If you want to make peace with your enemy, you have to work with your enemy. Then he becomes your partner."
-Nelson Mandela

"The Bible tells us to love our neighbors, and also to love our enemies; probably because generally they are the same people."
-G. K. Chesterton

We can demonize and we can humanize.

Amid the extreme dissension and tension of the 2016 Clinton vs. Trump presidential election, I came across a poster at a protest that stated, "I might disagree with you, but I'm pretty sure you're not Hitler." It is so easy to look at people different from us as something other than real, living, breathing, eating, sleeping, laughing, crying, loving, and hurting human beings. We see the other as a right-wing conservative, a bleeding-heart liberal, a deplorable, an illegal, a Republican, a Democrat, a Christian, and an atheist, or we pick from the hundreds of other ways in which we can identify and categorize ourselves and other human beings. Some of these are labels we are proud of, but they can quickly become a means to find ourselves justified in our thoughts, words or acts of incivility, separation, demonization, and dehumanization. We create clever and personally convincing ways to embody the words of the thought-provoking book by Nat Hentoff, *Free Speech for Me, but Not for Thee: How the American Left and Right Relentlessly Censor Each Other.*

Yet, there are countless moments in our lives when we encounter other people in ways that are free from such labels. We stop to help a person with a flat tire, or they do the same for us. We find ourselves holding the door for a person whose hands are full of groceries. We gesture to let a person into our lane on the highway. We find ourselves sitting beside a person in the emergency room waiting area, the subway, the airplane, or at the park bench while watching our children on the playground. In these moments, we often don't lead with labels and categories.

While sometimes visible or auditory signals quickly send us into a mode of labeling, there are so many precious moments in our lives when that isn't the case. These moments represent what is beautiful, important, and special about living in a diverse community, nation, and world. They are moments when we can see and recognize one another as fellow human beings.

Dehumanization is simply extracting the human qualities from a person. When we do this, we find it easier to justify ignoring, harming, and judging others in ways that would be challenging if we truly saw them as part of the human family. While there are horrifying and extreme instances used to justify everything from mass genocide to looking the other direction in the presence of such actions, subtle forms appear everywhere.

This quest is not only for you.

It is for your community, nation, and world. It is an invitation for all of us to see a better way and to see others in a new way.

I intentionally included this as one of the last challenges so that you could build up to it. Don't stop now. This quest calls for a kind of soul searching that is not easy. As it says in Proverbs 20:5, "Counsel in the heart of man is like deep water; but a man of understanding will draw it out." It is not easy to seek and understand the depth of our own motives and purposes, but there is wisdom and reward in doing so. With the added challenge and personal stretching come more amazing treasures and opportunities for personal growth and transformation.

The Quest

1. First, make a list of labels you use to diminish other people in your life, community, and world. This is going to be different for almost every person going on this quest. It might be prompted by your own biases and prejudices (we all have many). It might be informed by real and painful lived-experiences and encounters. Regardless,

create the list.

2. Unlike some of the other experiments, you are going to be quite narrow in your focus for this quest. Out of your list, choose one of these labels that you find yourself using (even if just in your own mind, things that you don't say out loud), one that you are ready and willing to explore on a deeper level.

3. Next, go to your calendar and schedule seven to ten consecutive days where you can commit a set time. If you have 15 minutes, then schedule that. If you want to explore more deeply, schedule 30 minutes or more. If your life and schedule allow, you can always block off and hour and finish early on some days.

4. When you get to the first scheduled day and time, you are simply going to explore and seek understanding. Turn to your favorite browser and start looking for people who fit the label or category you chose. Your task is to find one or more person each day and learn as much as possible about them during your daily allotted time. Try to get to know them as people – beyond the labels. What are their joys, fears, challenges, life history, hobbies, interests, and more? Look for things that you have in common.

5. As you search, write down things you learn about that person that extend beyond the label. Then, record what you have in common. Push yourself to seek understanding and not simply build reinforcement to further justify your views and

feelings toward people in this category. The key is to focus upon a particular person, which for practical purposes will probably be someone well-known, maybe even a celebrity.

6. This is a quest that benefits more than the others from creating time to briefly journal (even just bullet points) what you are learning and experiencing.

7. Repeat this process each day with a different person.

8. At the end, set aside extra time for a longer journal reflection. In addition, consider talking through what you learned with a trusted friend or family member.

Tips for the Journey

- Be honest with yourself. There is really no point in taking this quest if you are going to pretend. This quest offers incredible treasures, but it does demand genuine honesty, humility, and self-reflection.

- In your search for specific people, it is often helpful to choose people who are well-known but not well-known to you. You want to find and learn enough that you can begin to relate with the person beyond the surface.

- Avoid choosing names or people who are

especially polarizing. Consider going beyond the most extreme names that come to mind. It can be enlightening to expand your awareness beyond those few names.

- As you read and learn more, you will be tempted to gravitate toward the differences between you and information that supports your existing thoughts and emotions. I'm not asking you to change your personal beliefs and values, but I am inviting you to look beyond the most dividing elements. Try to see each person as a human. Look at how you can relate with this person, even if you must start with incredibly simple or self-evident factors.

- Remember that in these quests more is required. You are this far in the book, so that says something about your resolve and engagement with the process, but I'm absolutely convinced that these quests must begin with your choice to accept the call. If you are not ready, then don't go; or you can adjust the focus of the quest so that it stretches you but better aligns with the level of challenge that you are ready to face.

CHAPTER 11

THE NEW SONG QUEST

"One should, each day, try to hear a little song, read a good poem, see a fine picture, and, if possible, speak a few reasonable words."
-Goethe, Wilhelm Meister's Apprenticeship

When one of the most brilliant minds in history offers a few suggested daily habits, we are wise to listen and maybe even experiment with the suggestions.

If you look for lists of the greatest geniuses of all time, you almost always find Johann Wolfgang Goethe near the top. Goethe was a German novelist, poet, statesman, and scientist. He was a polymath whose work influenced Hegel, Kierkegaard, Nietzsche, Jung, Emerson, and Schopenhauer, to name a few. To truly appreciate his brilliance, most say that you must experience his writing in the original German. Some point to his written works as nearly flawless across the genres that he explored.

Goethe offers some advice for breathing more of the arts into your life. His words about daily habits do not actually come as personal advice from Goethe. Rather, they are drawn from one of the characters in his novel, *Wilhelm Meister's Apprenticeship*. In this book a young man of the 1700s is striving to escape the world of economics for a life as an actor and playwright. Within that context, we find the following advice: "One ought, every day at least, to hear a little song, read a good poem, see a fine picture, and if it were possible, to speak a few reasonable words."

Since Goethe first wrote these words, this brief statement has become a guide for many people throughout history. This statement became a proverb for breathing in life. Using the language of this book, it represents a treasure map. The treasures do not reveal themselves until we commit to embracing the advice of that line, until we explore what it is like to enjoy good music, poetry, art, and conversation on a daily basis. Maybe we go to an art museum on occasion. Perhaps we listen to music while exercising or during our morning commute. But what happens when you intentionally and consistently create space in your daily life to experience all of these things together?

This quest is an opportunity to explore this question for yourself.

"Art enables us to find ourselves and lose ourselves at the same time."
-Thomas Merton

The Quest

1. Set aside a journal to track your experiment and experiences on this quest. If you have a single journal that you are using to reflect and catalog all 12 quests, great. If not, consider dedicating one journal specifically for this quest.

2. You know yourself best, but consider blocking

off 15 minutes each day for at least seven days to conduct this experiment. Put it in your calendar.

3. Before you begin, invite respected friends, family, and others whom you respect to recommend their favorite songs, or the most beautiful songs they've ever heard. Ask them about a poem that inspired, moved, or intrigued them. Then invite them to share the same about a painting or other piece of art.

4. Your goal is to collect at least 10 songs, 10 poems, and 10 pieces of art.

5. For the next seven days, you are going to dedicate time to listen to one of the songs, read and ponder one of the poems, and view and ponder one of the pieces of art.

6. Record your thoughts and observations each day.

7. Then, talk about what you heard, read, or saw to at least one person each day. It doesn't need to be a long conversation. It might be a simple reference to what you are pondering, how it made you feel, what you observed, or questions that the song, poem, or art led you to consider.

8. At the end of the seven days, write a longer journal entry about what you learned and share your lessons with a friend or family member over coffee or lunch, or consider sharing it in a blog or other place where you connect with others online.

Tips for the Journey

- If you think this is too much for you, just do part of the experiment. Simplify and enjoy. Consistency and follow-through are important to uncovering the treasures within this quest. This is particularly important if you are someone who rarely listens to music, enjoys visual art, or reads poetry. As is true for many who enjoy coffee today, one's first cut is not necessarily the most desirable. There is an acquired taste that takes time to develop. This experiment is actually too short to develop such a taste, even if it is enough to give you a glimpse of what is possible.

- If you like to journal and write, you might write full paragraphs, but you might also create a daily bullet point list of questions and observations from each of these experiences. As with every quest, what you make of it, what you think about it, and how you savor it plays a large part in determining how much you get out of it.

- Talking about your experiment and lessons can be enriching, and I highly recommend it, but if it is too much to find someone each day, consider just doing it two or three times during the quest.

- Consider finding a partner or group to do it with you. You might find your own songs, poems, and art or come up with a common list as a group.

CHAPTER 12

THE FEAR QUEST

"The cave you fear to enter holds the treasure you seek."
-Joseph Campbell

I'm going to tell you something that you already know, but if you are like most people out there, you still struggle with it. It is like the healthcare professionals who know, better than most, the negative impact of a habit like smoking, standing outside and enduring frigid winter temperatures for a cigarette break. It is one thing to know something to be true, and it is another to turn that truth into a habit, or to use that truth to break a habit.

Fear is holding you back, and often not in a good way.

It plays a positive role in our lives. It can alert us to danger, prompting us to be cautious. But what happens when it doesn't just alert us to danger, and we let it take control of our decisions?

We constantly "play it safe" instead of mitigating risk and moving forward, instead of taking careful and calculated risks. We let fear amplify risks beyond what is real, leading us to hesitate, retreat, or run away from what could have been an awe-inspiring, life-changing moment or opportunity for us.

We can see fear as a gift but must not allow it to be the author of our life story. No grand quest ever came about by perpetually running away or hiding. Maybe the hero ran away and hid for a time, but eventually he had to take courage and change course. This is not about ridding ourselves of fear; it is about deciding how much we are willing to listen to it.

Some people might want to conquer every fear in their lives. They see any fear as a sign of weakness, as a deficiency or illness to be treated. Others choose to look at it more pragmatically.

Is fear keeping you from achieving your goals? Is it diminishing your sense of well-being? Does it lead you to behave in ways that are not in line with who you want to be or how you want to behave? Maybe the answer is "no." Maybe it is a fear of something that you rarely or never encounter in your life, and you are fine with that. In such situations, maybe it is just as well to not worry about it. Maybe someday, if you find yourself wanting or needing to act in a way that is inhibited by that fear, you can choose to do something about it. Maybe today isn't that day.

At the same time, there is also a type of fear that clinical psychologists define as a phobia, and it is diminishing your quality of life in some way. If you're dealing with this kind of fear, it might be wise to seek professional help. Psychologists offer a wide array of tools and strategies that many people find quite helpful.

If you are a human being, you have fears, and sometimes those fears get the best of you. They hold you back from goals. They distract. They might even diminish your sense of well-being. As you go about your *hero's journey* in life, these fears seek to undermine your efforts along the way.

"He who is not every day conquering some fear has not learned the secret of life."
-Ralph Waldo Emerson

To be clear, this is not about ignoring danger. That is foolish. We recognize real dangers. We assess risk. We prepare. We take necessary precautions. Yet, once we've done all that work and count the cost, we have the choice to make. Will we accept the call to the *hero's quest* and the risks associated with it, or will we fool ourselves into thinking that the safe route is the best path?

Out of all the quests in this book, this one, for some people, may be considered the most intimidating. It is a quest to face our fears, but more than that, it is about understanding our fears, learning about ourselves, and learning to take more of our life back, giving voice to our fears but not letting them dominate the conversation in each of our minds.

The Quest

1. Choose a fear that is holding you back, one that you are ready to explore. It is okay if you are not comfortable or ready to completely face the fear. For this quest, I'm simply inviting you to explore it, to learn more about it.

2. Next, get out your calendar and block off seven or ten days, allocating a specific 15 to 30-minute timeframe on each of these days.

3. Your mission is to simply use the dedicated time for each of these seven to ten days to learn more about, and better understand, your fear. You can choose when you want to do each, but the challenge is to accomplish three or more of the following during the days you set aside for the quest: (1) find and read at least five articles (from trusted sources, not just random online articles) about the fear you selected, (2) find and read (or skim) at least one book focused upon that fear, (3) read the story of at least three people who experienced and faced the fear, (4) interview or learn from at least one expert on the fear, and (5) document a list of the most effective strategies for facing this fear.

4. Each day, after doing your "research," write a brief journal entry detailing what you learned about the fear and what you learned about yourself.

5. On the last day or two of the challenge, decide what you want to do next. Come up with a plan

of action for yourself. Is it still important to you to face this fear? Do you have any strategies or ideas that you want to try? During the reading, if you found that you might want or need to seek professional help with the challenge, are you ready to reach out for that help? Maybe you'll decide that you learned enough, and you are fine setting this quest aside for now. No guilt here. You choose what you are ready for next.

Tips for the Journey

- Yes, this quest is ultimately about facing your fears, but it is just as much about exploring and understanding your relationship with a particular fear. It is also about discovering the simple power of gaining new knowledge.

- This is not a guilt quest. You have not failed if you still have the fear at the end, even if you decide that you don't want to devote the time or emotional energy to try and get rid of, or significantly reduce, this fear effect on you. Use this as a chance to learn more about the fear and about yourself. If you've done that, then you've successfully completed the quest.

- If you found this to be a helpful exercise, you can always apply it to another fear.

- A beautiful and unexpected part of this quest is cultivating a measure of humility and empathy for the fears and challenges for others. This is a wonderful theme to explore during your journaling for this quest.

CHAPTER 13

THE STORYTELLING QUEST

"Stories are a communal currency of humanity."
-Tahir Shah, in Arabian Nights

"Tell me the facts and I'll learn. Tell me the truth and I'll believe. But tell me a story and it will live in my heart forever."
-Native American Proverb

Your life is a story. It is an incredible, unpredictable, beautiful, painful, and joyful story, only you can't skip ahead to find out how it ends. You are writing it as you are living it.

Your life is a collection of wonderful and connected short stories. Each story contributes to the larger one. This collection of stories is fascinating and complex. You are one of many characters in this story, and it is often impossible to tell where your story ends and another person's story begins. That is okay. In fact, it is beautiful.

As a human, you are designed to crave stories. They are an important means by which you make sense of your life, the world, and your place in that world. While these stories are unpredictable in nature, you can contribute to the meaning found in that story. Even in a story of tragedy, you can choose to seek, discover, and savor its meaning.

You don't celebrate the tragedy. Celebrate that you are in it, and that you have discovered meaning and purpose in times of tragedy and triumph. For those who consider themselves people of faith, you can also celebrate and stand in awe of the fact that your story is, in fact, part of an even grander story.

Not only is your life a collection of stories, but the stories around you are a rich source of meaning and learning. You learn by listening to the stories of others. You explore, empathize, celebrate, grieve, and grow. Perhaps this is why so many people spend their free time immersed in stories – films, television shows, songs, novels …

As we experience stories, we find ourselves connected to something that we crave as humans. At the same time, many of us hide our stories. We keep them to ourselves, perhaps only sharing them with a few close friends and family members.

Sharing your stories is a gift to people, a gift to the world.

People learn by hearing your story.

They are moved to think and sometimes act in new ways. Even when you don't realize it, the simple gift of telling a story from your life can move and inspire people in amazing ways. You invite them to imagine something new, something beyond their own sphere of experience. In other cases, you remind them that they are not alone, that their story and your story are much more connected than they ever realized.

With this in mind, here is the last quest. It is a quest of telling some of your stories to others. This involves risk and vulnerability, but that is true with any gift that you offer to another person.

This last quest is, in some ways, not a quest. It is the part of the quest where you return home. After overcoming incredible adversity, gaining new knowledge and skill, discovering amazing treasures, and experiencing potentially transformational life lessons, you've returned.

Now what?

Now is the time to rest, reflect, and tell others about your story. In doing so, you are offering them a glimpse into your own quests and an invitation to start their own.

The Quest

1. While a specific number of days is not essential for this quest, I encourage you to choose some sort of time frame. Perhaps stick with the common seven to ten-day range. Block it off on your calendar, allocating the amount of time that you have available.

2. Reflect and revisit your recorded and unrecorded experiences and lessons as a collection of related stories. If you want, you can write them out. Or, consider creating an outline for each story as if you were preparing to present it to a large audience of people. Actually create the outline

and practice talking about these stories. Practice in private or with trusted people around you.

3. When you are ready, your challenge is to start telling these stories. Don't just force them upon people but look for opportunities. If you prefer something more formal, you can invite someone to lunch and ask if they are willing to let you reflect out loud and share what you have experienced and learned.

4. That might be all there is to this quest, but the difference for this one is that it doesn't end. Keep these stories. Continue sharing them and talking about them with others. As you do, you will often find yourself learning even more about who you are, with new lessons surfacing after the fact.

Tips for the Journey

- Yes, this quest is about you, getting comfortable as a storyteller and further reflecting on the experiences and lessons from your quests. Remember that this is about others as well. You may not expect that sharing your story can or will make a difference in the listeners' lives, but it might. Sometimes you will see it, or the person hearing your story will explicitly tell you how they were influenced. Maybe it will remain a mystery. Either is fine. Simply embrace your role as a teller of good stories, a person willing to share a bit of your life with others.

- Practicing telling your stories might seem formal or even inauthentic. I invite you to try it. This process of practice and rehearsal has some surprise treasures and life lessons of its own, ones that I leave to you to discover.

- As you tell your stories, you will often find yourself adding or adjusting what you say and how you say it. Embrace that. Even as you share your story, you are engaging in a sort of ongoing editing and re-writing that is making the lessons an even more integrated part of your life.

CONCLUSION

Congratulations!

If you've gotten this far, it is likely that one of three things has occurred. One is that you've completed all the quests and you are now here at the end. Another is that you finished some of the quests and decided to check out the ending, maybe even just because you've been trained to always read the last few pages of any book. The other possibility is that you just skipped the entire introduction and other 12 chapters, going right to the conclusion.

If you are in that last category, I hate to disappoint you, but there are no grand conclusions or treasures for you in this chapter. The grand conclusions and treasures are reserved for those who completed one or more of the quests. As I mentioned at the beginning of this book, this is more of a treasure map than it is a book, and simply looking at a treasure map has limited value. The real excitement happens when you use the treasure map to embark on a grand adventure.

If you are in one of those first two categories, I offer you deep and sincere congratulations. Thank you for trusting me and this book to serve as a guide. I am humbled and honored that you have accepted the calls to quests offered in this book. It is my genuine hope and prayer that you find yourself in possession of new and potentially profound treasures from your journeys.

If You Remember One Thing

We rarely remember most of what we read in books. For an average book, it is good if you can recall 15 or 20 percent of the content in six months. This book is different. It will be different for you. That is because the most important lessons are not in the book. The most important lessons are the ones that you experienced by going on one or more of the quests. You might not remember what I wrote in the chapter on wonder, but I guarantee that you will remember that sunrise or sunset for years, even decades.

Maybe you will not remember the details of what I wrote in the chapter about savoring, but if you truly accepted the call and went on the savoring and sharing quest, an important part of that experience will be with you for life. The same is true for every one of these quests, and this points to the single most important lesson in the book. If you embrace this one lesson moving forward, your life will be qualitatively different. You will experience a richness and depth that may well have been absent before.

What is that one lesson?

Don't just read about life, live it.

Experience, experiment, learn, grow, and embrace life as a series of quests. Life change and transformation happens when you act and reflect. I'm convinced that this is why we so often remain unhappy with the outcomes of many schools today. Even while people are striving to bring about reform and change, much of education is still fixated on facts and information. Information is good. We live in a world where more information is available to you through a click of a mouse than was available to a person of the 12th century in a hundred lifetimes.

However, wisdom and richness only come when you take some of that information and act upon it. It is when you take that idea and give it flesh and bones, when you bring it into your life through experience. As the musician Charlie Peacock once wrote in a song, "You can only possess what you experience." The lesson is to learn by doing. Take any new knowledge or information and ask these questions. How can I experiment with this in my life? What would happen if I turned this into a real-world quest?

If you remember this one lesson, if you choose to embrace learning through simple life experiments and quests, then my task will have been accomplished. Even if you forget everything else that I wrote, it is my hope that you remember – that you act upon this one lesson.

What is the alternative? I suppose you can try to forget the rich and rewarding experiences that came from these quests, that you can remain committed to the idea that collecting as much knowledge and content as possible will make your life better in some way. You can strive to remain a consumer of content without stepping into the incredible journey of being a creator of life-moments and experiences. If you choose this path, I wish you the best.

To tell the truth, I think that is an unlikely outcome. Once you've begun to experience the treasures of a quest-based approach to life, it is hard to turn back.

What's Next?

Many of these quests, while timebound, are invitations to new ways of thinking, doing, and being. There is always more to learn and do. Maybe you will decide to repeat some of the quests. Perhaps you are ready to start creating some of your own personal quests. If you're not ready to do that, consider this:

This book is intended to be the first in a series of 12.

While the other books in the series will each be designed for specific audiences to be determined (leaders, teens, innovators, parents, etc.), I'm confident that one or more of the forthcoming books will fit your life situation.

Just don't wait for another book. There are so many more quests to be pursued and written. Now that you've seen and acquired the many treasures, I suspect that you have a new and growing appetite for more. With that in mind, I conclude this book with the blessing that I shared with you at the beginning:

"As you head out on these quests, may each new treasure leave you blessed. May your adventure be full of mystery and meaning, wonder and play. May truth, beauty, and goodness come to you each day. And may you have the eyes to see that all of these are merely glimpses of treasures in eternity."

Made in the USA
Middletown, DE
25 September 2019